Sentence & Paragraph Construction

by Samantha L. Stuart

TABLE OF CONTENTS

This book is designed to introduce or review the skills required to write sentences and paragraphs. Explanations of the concepts are included, but the main focus is on student practice. Engaging activities help students understand that writing is an important communication tool. You can use the pages that focus on skills your students need to develop, or you can use the pages sequentially to give students a comprehensive review of various sentence and paragraph types. (Page 28 is a review page that can also be used as a pretest to gauge students' familiarity with the concepts covered in this book.)

Answers

Page 1
1. subject: I
   predicate: enjoy writing in my journal
2. subject: My brother Joe
   predicate: won a writing contest last year
3. subject: Brittany and Brianna
   predicate: are in the same English class
4. subject: Anthony
   predicate: writes funny stories on the computer
5. subject: Our teacher
   predicate: displays our best writing on the bulletin board behind her desk
6. subject: (implied) You
   predicate: Write an essay about the American Revolution

7-11. Answers will vary.

Page 2
2. Every night I go to my room at 9 p.m. I stay awake reading until after 10:00 p.m.
3. Alan has to complete his term paper tonight. He won't have time to go to the soccer game tomorrow.

Sentences for 4 through 6 may vary slightly from the following.

4. Joe has gone scuba diving seven times, but I never have.
5. Our cat must have more than nine lives, because he's already lived at least ten.
6. My Aunt Mary usually beats me at chess, but sometimes she lets me win.
7. Answers will vary.
8. Answers will vary.

Page 3
Sentences may vary slightly from the following.

1. F—The sound of loud music gives me a headache.
2. R—My friend Matt plays the guitar. He's really good at playing the electric guitar.
3. R—Jordan is a great singer. Someday I think she'll be in a famous band.
4. F—The band looked wonderful marching onto the football field in their colorful uniforms.
5. R—Drums are my favorite instrument. Mom won't let me practice in the house.
6. F—My favorite bands are Upside Down, Crying Babies, and Speed Readers.
7. F—Back in the "olden days" when my parents were teenagers, clothing was very different.

Page 4
Sentences will vary.

Page 5
Sentences for 1 through 5 will vary.
6. Subject: paint
7. IMP
8. Subject: Pete
9. Subject: Maria
10. IMP
11. IMP
12. Subject: you

Page 6
Answers for 1 through 3 will vary.
Questions for 4 through 7 will vary. The following are sample questions.
4. What did you get for your birthday?
5. What are you doing this weekend?
6. Why do you look so tired?
7. Why are you wearing that silly hat?

Page 7
1. IMP, period
2. INT, question mark
3. E (or D), exclamation point (or period)
4. D, period
5. D, period
6. INT, question mark
7. IMP (or E), period (or exclamation point)

Sentences for 8 through 15 will vary.

Page 8
Sentences will vary. Make sure students use each method of combining sentences at least twice.
1. The average male blue whale is as long as a basketball court, and the females are even longer.
2. An average baby whale weighs as much as a full-grown elephant and will double its weight in one month.
3. Every summer, blue whales gather to feed near the coast of California.

4. Whales need to breathe air, so they swim to the surface of the water.
5. Killer whales are black and white and have fins on their backs.
6. Life isn't easy for teenage killer whales because they have to baby-sit their younger siblings.

Page 9
Sentences will vary.

Page 10
Sentences will vary.

Page 11
1. Charles Dickens wrote *A Tale of Two Cities*.
2. The governor gave a very interesting speech about education.
3. Too much television and not enough studying can cause bad grades.
4. The singer performed a beautiful rendition of "The Star Spangled Banner."
5. Someone painted the house.
6. I did the artwork displayed on the hall bulletin board.
7. Someone driving a black van delivered the package.
8. Someone restored the classic car to its original color.
9. Someone wishing to remain anonymous wrote this letter.

Page 12
Students' paragraphs will vary but should include a topic sentence and supporting details from the outline. The following is a sample paragraph.

The Statue of Liberty is a symbol of freedom that was given to the U.S. as a gift from France. All of the money for the statue was donated by the people of France. They wanted it to be a gift for America's centennial, but it was not completed on time. Frederic Auguste Bartholdi was the sculptor who designed the statue. The 151-foot iron frame was completed by the French engineer Gustave Eiffel. The Statue of Liberty was completed in Paris in 1884, but it wasn't unveiled in New York Harbor until 1886. The United States supplied the base the statue now rests on.

Page 13
1. a
2. b
3. c
4. b

Page 14
Topic Sentences will vary. The following are sample topic sentences.
1. Today was not a good day.
2. Jai alai is an unusual sport.
3. It seems like sharks are invincible.
4. I really enjoy Grandma's Sunday visits.
5. The pipe organ is a complicated instrument.

Page 15
Sentences will vary. The following are sample sentences.
1. The Service Club meets every Tuesday afternoon.
2. My brother usually helps me with my science homework.
3. If it doesn't rain before Saturday, the river will be too low for us to go rafting.
4. She learned to roll over at a very early age.

Page 16
Paragraphs will vary. Note that students will need to use their work on this page to complete page 18.

Page 17
Paragraphs will vary. Make sure students can identify which strategy they used to organize the information in their paragraph.

Page 18
Paragraphs will vary. Compare the paragraphs completed for this page to those completed for page 16 to make sure students have made effective revisions.

Page 19
Causes and effects will vary. The following are sample answers.
Causes: poor time management, a family emergency, forgetting about the assignment, illness
Effects: low grade, punishment from parents, punishment from teacher, anxiety
Students' paragraphs will vary.

Page 20

Answers will vary.

Page 21

Paragraphs will vary.

Page 22

Answers will vary.

Page 23

Answers will vary.

Page 24

Paragraphs will vary.

Page 25

Answers will vary.

Page 26

Answers will vary.

Page 27

This page reviews many of the major concepts presented in this book.

1. explanatory
2. "War" is a card game that involves several steps.
3. declarative
4. The following sentences are in the passive voice: *First, a standard deck of cards is divided in half. Each of two players is given 26 cards. Three cards are added facedown by each player. Then a fourth card is turned over.*
5. One of the sentences in the passive voice should be written as follows: *First, divide a standard deck of cards in half. Give each of two players 26 cards. Each player adds three cards facedown. Each player turns over a fourth card.*
6. Answers will vary.
7. Sentences will vary. Make sure students correctly combined the two sentences they identified for question 6.
8. Sentences will vary.

Page 28

1. h
2. m
3. c
4. i
5. g
6. j
7. e
8. a
9. l
10. n
11. k
12. b
13. f
14. d

Name _____

Writing a Simple Sentence

A **simple sentence** is a group of words that expresses one complete thought. It has a subject (a person or thing that is being or doing) and a predicate (the part of the sentence that tells what the subject is or does).

subj. pred.
Example: My pencil fell onto the floor.

All the words related to the subject make up the **complete subject**. All the words related to the predicate make up the **complete predicate**.

comp. subj. comp. pred.
Example: My pencil fell onto the floor.

Note: Sometimes the subject of a simple sentence is *implied,* not stated. In the following example, the subject *You* is not part of the sentence, but it is implied.
Example: (You) Wash the car.

In each of the following simple sentences, underline the complete subject and circle the complete predicate.

1. I enjoy writing in my journal.

2. My brother Joe won a writing contest last year.

3. Brittany and Brianna are in the same English class.

4. Anthony writes funny stories on the computer.

5. Our teacher displays our best writing on the bulletin board behind her desk.

6. Write an essay about the American Revolution.

On the lines below, write five simple sentences about the picture. Remember that each of your sentences should express a complete thought. When you've finished writing, underline your complete subjects and circle your complete predicates.

7. _____

8. _____

9. _____

10. _____

11. _____

Writing a Compound Sentence

A **compound sentence** is made up of two simple sentences joined by a comma and a connecting word such as *or*, *but*, *because*, or *and*.

Example: My pencil fell onto the floor, but John picked it up for me.

Separate each of the following compound sentences into two simple sentences. The first one has been done for you.

1. Allison likes to play with dolls, but her twin sister prefers trucks. *Allison likes to play with dolls. Her twin sister prefers trucks.*

2. Every night I go to my room at 9 p.m., but I stay awake reading until after 10:00 p.m. _____

3. Alan has to complete his term paper tonight, or he won't have time to go to the soccer game tomorrow._____
_____

Combine each of the following pairs of simple sentences into a compound sentence. Be sure to include a comma and a connecting word in each compound sentence.

4. Joe has gone scuba diving seven times. I never have. _____
_____

5. Our cat must have more than nine lives. He's already lived at least ten. _____
_____

6. My Aunt Mary usually beats me at chess. Sometimes she lets me win. _____
_____

7. Open any book and look for compound sentences. On the lines below, list two of the compound sentences you find. Circle the connecting word in each compound sentence.

_____
_____
_____

8. Write two compound sentences about what you are planning to do next weekend. Circle the connecting word in each of your compound sentences.

_____
_____
_____

Correcting Sentence Fragments and Run-ons

Just because a group of words begins with a capital letter and ends with a period doesn't mean it's a complete sentence. Sometimes what appears to be a sentence is actually a sentence fragment or a run-on sentence.

Remember that a simple sentence has a subject and a predicate. A **sentence fragment** is missing one or both of these.

> Example: *Likes running through the field on summer mornings. (missing subject)*
> Example: *Our energetic dog Pepper. (missing predicate)*
> Example: *Sometimes on summer mornings. (missing subject and predicate)*

A **run-on sentence** is two or more sentences that run together without proper punctuation. Often you cannot tell where one thought ends and the next begins.

> Example: *Sometimes on summer mornings our energetic dog Pepper likes running through the fields he loves to play fetch.*

Each of the following groups of words is either a sentence fragment or a run-on sentence. Write F on the line before each fragment, and R on the line before each run-on. Make each group of words into one or more complete sentences by adding information to the fragments and splitting the run-ons into separate sentences.

1. _____ The sound of loud music.

_____

2. _____ My friend Matt plays the guitar he's really good at playing the electric guitar.

_____

3. _____ Jordan is a great singer someday I think she'll be in a famous band.

_____

4. _____ Marching onto the football field in their colorful uniforms.

_____

5. _____ Drums are my favorite instrument Mom won't let me practice in the house.

_____

6. _____ My favorite bands Upside Down, Crying Babies, and Speed Readers.

_____

7. _____ Back in the "olden days" when my parents were teenagers.

_____

Writing a Declarative Sentence

There are several different types of sentences. Each type is used for a different communication purpose. A sentence that simply makes a statement is called a **declarative sentence**. This type of sentence ends with a period.

Example: My language arts notebook is yellow.

Answer each of the following questions with a simple declarative sentence.

1. What color is your language arts notebook?

_____

2. How do you feel when you get an A on a test?

_____

3. Do you have a big family or a small one?

_____

4. What is your favorite subject in school?

_____

5. What is your favorite weekend activity?

_____

Answer each of the following questions with a compound declarative sentence. Remember that a compound sentence is made up of two simple sentences joined by a comma and a connecting word such as or, but, or and.

Example: Do you have any siblings?
I don't have any brothers or sisters, but I do have eight cousins.

6. Have you ever gone ice skating?

_____

_____

7. Do you enjoy spending time with small children?

_____

_____

8. What time are you supposed to turn out your light?

_____

_____

9. Do you have a computer in your home?

_____

_____

Writing an Imperative Sentence

An **imperative sentence** makes a request or gives a command. This type of sentence ends with a period or an exclamation point.

Example: Please hand me that paintbrush.

Imagine you are in an art class. Write five imperative sentences you might hear.

1. _____
2. _____
3. _____
4. _____
5. _____

Remember that the subject of a sentence can be implied rather than stated. The subject of an imperative sentence is always *you*, even if a name is mentioned.

Example: (Would you) Please hand me that paintbrush.
Example: Steven, (would you) please hand me that paintbrush.

Write IMP on the line in front of each sentence below that is imperative. Underline the subject in the sentences that are not imperative. Hint: For questions, think about who or what is performing the action.

6. _____ The paint spilled!

7. _____ Make sure you don't forget to shade in the petals.

8. _____ Has Pete ever taken pottery classes?

9. _____ Maria is great with paint, but she doesn't know how to use chalk yet.

10. _____ Anna, get Derek a cup of water so he can rinse his brushes.

11. _____ Wash your hands and clean your supplies before the bell rings.

12. _____ What talented artists you are!

Writing an Exclamatory Sentence

An **exclamatory sentence** expresses strong emotion. This type of sentence ends with an exclamation point.

Example: This is the best cheesecake I've ever tasted!

The following pairs of sentences may appear to be the same at first glance, but look carefully at the punctuation. For each pair, describe a situation when you might use or hear sentence A (declarative) and a situation when you might use or hear sentence B (exclamatory). It might help to read the sentences aloud using a different tone of voice for each type of sentence.

1. A. I need help. *when I can't figure out a math problem* _____
    B. I need help! _____

2. A. This is terrible. _____
    B. This is terrible! _____

3. A. I forgot. _____
    B. I forgot! _____

Writing an Interrogative Sentence

An **interrogative sentence** asks a question. This type of sentence ends with a question mark.

Example: Have you ever been to see the Statue of Liberty?

Read each declarative sentence below and then write a question (interrogative sentence) that could be answered by that declarative sentence.

4. I received a red bicycle for my birthday. _____

5. Our neighborhood is having a yard sale this weekend. _____
    _____

6. The baby in the apartment above ours was crying all night. _____
    _____

7. The hairdresser wasn't paying attention when she cut my bangs. _____
    _____

Name _____

Reviewing Sentence Types

There are four types of sentences. Each type is used for a different communication purpose.
- A **declarative sentence** makes a statement. It ends with a period.
- An **interrogative sentence** asks a question. It ends with a question mark.
- An **imperative sentence** makes a request or gives a command. It ends with a period or an exclamation point.
- An **exclamatory sentence** expresses strong emotion. It ends with an exclamation point.

Label each of the following sentences as declarative **(D)**, *interrogative* **(INT)**, *imperative* **(IMP)**, *or exclamatory* **(E)**. *Also add the correct punctuation to each sentence.*

1. _____ Please water the garden tonight since I won't be home

2. _____ Do you think I should plant carrots or tomatoes

3. _____ These roses are gorgeous

4. _____ I have zinnias, roses, pansies, and petunias in my flower garden

5. _____ Working in the garden is relaxing and enjoyable for me

6. _____ How do you know when carrots are ready to be picked

7. _____ Don't let your pet rabbit get into my garden

On each line below, write a sentence you might hear at a construction site. Before you begin, think about what the construction workers might say to one another.

8. (declarative) _____

9. (declarative) _____

10. (interrogative) _____

11. (interrogative) _____

12. (imperative) _____

13. (imperative) _____

14. (exclamatory) _____

15. (exclamatory) _____

Combining Sentences

Effective writing includes sentences of varying lengths. Often two short, related sentences can be combined to create a longer sentence. You've already learned how to make a compound sentence out of two simple sentences by using a comma and a conjunction. With this method of combining sentences, no words are lost.

Simple sentences: My pencil fell onto the floor. John picked it up for me.
Compound sentence: My pencil fell onto the floor, but John picked it up for me.

You can also combine two related sentences by rearranging some words. Some words may be added and some may be left out, but the same ideas are expressed.

Simple sentences: I wrote an essay for my history class. It was on World War II.
Combined sentence: I wrote an essay about World War II for my history class.

Simple sentences: I like tangerines. I also like oranges.
Combined sentence: I like tangerines and oranges.

Combine each of the following pairs of sentences to make one longer sentence. Use each method described above at least twice.

1. An average male blue whale is as long as a basketball court. The females are even longer. _____

   _____

2. An average baby whale weighs as much as a full-grown elephant. It will double its weight in one month. _____

   _____

3. Every summer, blue whales gather near the coast of California. They feed there.

   _____

4. Whales need to breathe air. They swim to the surface of the water.

   _____

5. Killer whales are black and white. They have fins on their backs.

   _____

6. Life isn't easy for teenage killer whales. They have to baby-sit their younger siblings. _____

   _____

Expanding Sentences

Expanding sentences sometimes gives a reader additional information and can make sentences more descriptive.

Short sentence: The juice spilled.

Expanded sentence: The dark purple grape juice spilled across the table and onto the snow-white carpet.

Make these sentences more descriptive by adding adjectives, adverbs, and prepositional phrases.

1. The car stopped. _____

    _____

2. We ate potatoes. _____

    _____

3. The puppy jumped. _____

    _____

4. Ed swam. _____

    _____

5. I wrote. _____

    _____

6. The elephant walked. _____

    _____

7. I ripped the paper. _____

    _____

8. The ice cream melted. _____

    _____

9. Emma laughed. _____

    _____

10. The candles flickered. _____

    _____

Expanding Sentences (continued)

All of the sentences in a paragraph should work together to present ideas in a clear and interesting way. Combining and expanding shorter sentences can sometimes help avoid repetition and make a paragraph more interesting; however, a writer has to be careful not to change or leave out any necessary information contained in the original sentences.

1. On the lines below, write ten short sentences about things you like to do.

_____   _____

_____   _____

_____   _____

_____   _____

_____   _____

2. Create a few longer sentences by combining some of the sentences above that are closely related.

_____

_____

_____

_____

_____

3. Add adjectives, adverbs, and prepositional phrases to your sentences to make them as descriptive as possible.

_____

_____

_____

_____

_____

_____

_____

_____

_____

_____

Writing in the Active Voice

The **voice** of a sentence depends on whether the subject performs the action of the verb or receives the action of the verb. If the subject performs the action, the sentence is in the **active voice**. If the subject receives the action, the sentence is in the **passive voice**.

Active voice: Alan rode his bicycle.

Passive voice: The bicycle was ridden by Alan.

Many sentences in the passive voice contain the word *by*. As a general rule, sentences in the active voice are more effective. Try to use the active voice when writing sentences.

Rewrite the following sentences so that they are in the active voice.

1. *A Tale of Two Cities* was written by Charles Dickens.

_____

2. A very interesting speech about education was given by the governor.

_____

3. Bad grades can be caused by too much television and not enough studying.

_____

4. A beautiful rendition of "The Star Spangled Banner" was performed by the singer.

_____

5. The house has been painted. *(Hint: Use the word "someone" as the subject.)*

_____

6. The artwork displayed on the hall bulletin board was done by me.

_____

7. The package was delivered by someone driving a black van.

_____

8. The classic car has been restored to its original color. *(Hint: Use the word "someone" as the subject.)*

_____

9. This letter was written by someone wishing to remain anonymous.

_____

What Is a Paragraph?

A **paragraph** is a group of sentences that develop a main idea. The main idea is usually expressed in a **topic sentence**. The rest of the sentences in a paragraph contain supporting details. Supporting details provide explanations, facts, examples, or statistics that back up the main idea.

The following outline contains information for a paragraph about the Statue of Liberty. On the lines beneath the outline, write a paragraph by using the information provided. Read the whole outline before writing your topic sentence. Then use some of the remaining information to write complete sentences that support your topic sentence.

The Statue of Liberty

I. A Symbol of Freedom
  A. gift from France
    1. funds for statue donated by people of France
    2. they wanted to give a gift in 1876, on the anniversary of America's independence (but the statue wasn't completed on time)
  B. designers
    1. statue designed by French sculptor Frederic Auguste Bartholdi
    2. framework designed by French engineer Gustave Eiffel
  C. construction
    1. completed in Paris in 1884
    2. nearly 151 feet tall
    3. copper shell on outside, iron frame inside
  D. unveiling
    1. unveiled in New York Harbor in 1886
    2. base supplied by United States

_____

_____

_____

_____

_____

_____

_____

_____

_____

Name _____

Writing a Topic Sentence

A **topic sentence** expresses the main idea of a paragraph. All of the other sentences in the paragraph support and develop the main idea. The topic sentence is usually, but not always, the first sentence in the paragraph.

Circle the letter of the best topic sentence for each of the following sets of supporting details. Remember that the topic sentence is usually the first sentence in the paragraph.

1. For one thing, writing on the computer is a lot faster than writing on paper. Computers also allow writers to delete, move, or change information very easily. Computer spelling and grammar checkers help people make sure their writing is error-free.

   a. Computers have helped make writing easier.
   b. Spelling checkers are helpful.
   c. Writing is faster on the computer than on paper.

2. Various shades of glass are cut to fit a pattern. Thin strips of lead are then placed between the glass pieces and soldered together. The stained glass panel can then be hung in a window frame.

   a. Glass comes in many colors.
   b. Making stained glass windows involves several steps.
   c. Lead strips hold the stained glass together.

3. Penguins use their wings as flippers and their webbed feet and stiff tail as rudders. Like dolphins, they can leap out of the water at up to 25 miles per hour. Some penguins can even dive 850 feet below the water's surface to search for food.

   a. Penguins have to dive very deeply below the water's surface to find food.
   b. Penguins are similar to dolphins.
   c. Penguins are powerful swimmers.

4. Every year my grandparents have a delicious barbecue in their backyard, which is near a big lake. My cousins and I take a rowboat out to the middle of the lake, where we have an awesome view of the fireworks. Then we row back to the house to light sparklers and eat watermelon.

   a. Watermelon is a great summer snack.
   b. The Fourth of July is one of my favorite holidays.
   c. Fireworks look especially pretty over a lake.

Writing a Topic Sentence (continued)

Remember that a topic sentence expresses the main idea of a paragraph. Write a topic sentence for each of the following paragraphs.

1. _____.

   First, my math teacher gave us a pop quiz. Then I split my pants when I bent over to pick up everything that had fallen from the lunch tray I had dropped on the cafeteria floor. When I finally arrived home from school, a mile-long list of chores was waiting for me on the kitchen table. After all of my chores were done, I sat down to watch my favorite show on television. The cable was out.

2. _____.

   It is a form of handball. Jai alai is played on a court that has one or three walls. Players use a curved wicker basket to catch and return the small rubber ball to each other. It is a fast-paced and sometimes hazardous sport.

3. _____.

   There are more than 350 species of sharks. They can be found at all depths in all the oceans of the world (except the Antarctic). Even some freshwater lakes and rivers are home to sharks. Sharks have no enemies except other sharks, and very few diseases affect them.

4. _____.

   She brings double fudge chocolate chip cookies every time she comes to visit. Grandma tells the best stories about what her life was like when she was growing up. She listens to all my problems and gives me great advice. I look forward to our Sunday visits with her.

5. _____.

   The pipe organ produces its sound when air is blown through pipes of graduated sizes. The bottoms of the pipes are set on a box called the "wind chest." A system of valves in the wind chest, controlled by the keyboard player, allows air from the wind supply to enter the pipes and create their sound.

Writing Supporting Details

Supporting details provide facts, examples, statistics, or explanations that back up the main idea expressed in the topic sentence.

For each topic sentence below, write at least three sentences that contain supporting details.

1. **Topic Sentence:** There are many opportunities to participate in extracurricular activities at school.

   Supporting Details: _____

   _____

   _____

   _____

2. **Topic Sentence:** Having a brother can be a pain sometimes, but it has its advantages.

   Supporting Details: _____

   _____

   _____

   _____

3. **Topic Sentence:** The weather could affect our camping trip.

   Supporting Details: _____

   _____

   _____

   _____

4. **Topic Sentence:** Maggie is the most talented baby I have ever seen.

   Supporting Details: _____

   _____

   _____

   _____

Writing a Good Paragraph

A topic sentence, supporting details, and a concluding statement are often all included in a good paragraph.

An effective strategy for writing a paragraph is to state what you are going to say (topic sentence), say it (supporting details), and then briefly summarize what you've said (concluding statement).

Not all paragraphs require a concluding statement, but sometimes it is effective to restate the main idea or summarize the supporting details. Concluding statements are especially appropriate in essays or research papers.

On the lines below, write a paragraph about one of the following topics:

a favorite pet, life in your hometown, a family tradition

Be sure to include a topic sentence, at least five supporting details, and a concluding statement. You may want to brainstorm or outline on the back of this paper before you begin writing the paragraph.

_____

_____

_____

_____

_____

_____

_____

_____

_____

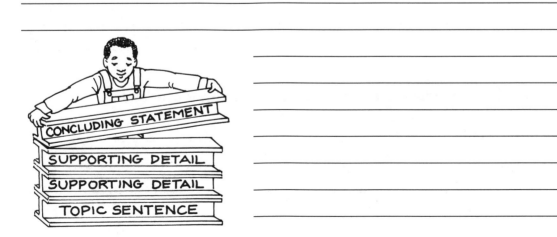

_____

_____

_____

_____

_____

_____

_____

Ordering Information in a Paragraph

There are many ways to organize the information in a paragraph, such as chronologically (time order), from most important to least important, or by working up to the most important information. You should choose the order that is most logical and effective for the type of information you will present in your paragraph.

Look at the pictures below. Write a paragraph about the pictures, organizing the information by using one of the strategies described above.

_____

_____

_____

_____

_____

_____

_____

_____

_____

_____

_____

_____

_____

_____

_____

_____

Revising a Paragraph

After you've written the first draft of a paragraph, you will want to revise it. The process of revision includes making improvements and any necessary corrections.
- Eliminate fragments and run-on sentences.
- Include various sentence types.
- Vary sentence length.
- Make sure all sentences are in the active voice.
- Make sure the sentence order is logical.

As you are revising, you also want to be sure your paragraph is as interesting and informative as possible. Think about the construction of a building. A building's structure could be perfect, yet the building could be dull. It needs decoration! Paragraphs are the same way. They need some "decoration" to make them as interesting as possible. Sensory details, imagery, and facts can all add interest to an ordinary paragraph.

Look back at the paragraph you wrote on page 16. Be sure the structure of the paragraph is correct. Then make the paragraph more interesting by adding sensory details, imagery, and facts wherever possible. Write the revised version of your paragraph on the lines below.

_____

_____

_____

_____

_____

_____

_____

_____

_____

_____

_____

_____

_____

_____

Name _____

Writing a Cause and Effect Paragraph

Just as there are different types of sentences for different communication purposes, there are different types of paragraphs.

A **cause and effect paragraph** presents the reasons for certain results or consequences. Sometimes the effect is stated in the topic sentence, and the causes are then discussed in the supporting sentences. At other times, a cause is stated in the topic sentence, and the effects are discussed in the supporting sentences.

List several possible causes for not completing a major writing project on time. Then list several possible effects of not completing the assignment on time.

Possible Causes	**Possible Effects**
_____	_____
_____	_____
_____	_____
_____	_____
_____	_____
_____	_____

Now write a cause and effect paragraph that discusses the consequences of one cause you listed above, or the causes of one effect you listed above. Make sure you include a topic sentence.

_____

_____

_____

_____

_____

_____

_____

_____

_____

_____

_____

_____

Name _____

Writing a Comparison/Contrast Paragraph

A **comparison/contrast paragraph** discusses the similarities and/or the differences between two things or ideas. Comparisons are made when similarities between things or ideas are presented. Contrasts are made when differences between things or ideas are presented. At least three differences or similarities between items or ideas should be included in a comparison/contrast paragraph.

Choose one of the following pairs for this activity. Circle the pair you have chosen.

parents/children, boys/girls, keyboard/pen, your room/family room

In the columns below, list several similarities and several differences between the people or things in the pair you have chosen.

Similarities	Differences
_____	_____
_____	_____
_____	_____
_____	_____
_____	_____

Now write a comparison/contrast paragraph that discusses either the similarities or differences (or both) between the people or things in the pair you selected. Be sure to include a topic sentence and at least three supporting sentences.

_____

_____

_____

_____

_____

_____

_____

_____

_____

_____

_____

_____

Writing a Descriptive Paragraph

A **descriptive paragraph** helps the reader clearly imagine what is being described. The use of details and accurate adjectives helps the writer create "imagery," descriptive language that appeals to the senses.

Your attitude towards your subject affects the details you choose to include in a descriptive paragraph. For example, a frog would be described quite differently by a person who is delighted to see it than by a person who is frightened of it.

1. Imagine you are watching the sun rise. Write a descriptive paragraph using vivid details and adjectives so that the reader can "see" the sun rising too.

_____

_____

_____

_____

_____

_____

_____

_____

_____

_____

_____

2. Keep in mind that descriptive language can appeal to any of the senses. Now write a paragraph that vividly describes the sound of a certain type of music. First, take a moment to consider your attitude about this type of music. Your attitude will influence the way you describe it.

_____

_____

_____

_____

_____

_____

_____

Writing an Informative Paragraph

> An **informative paragraph** gives the reader facts about a person, event, or any other topic. All of the paragraphs in a news article are informative.

Think about an event that you recently witnessed.

1. What happened? _____
   _____

2. When did this happen? _____

3. Who was involved? _____

4. Why did this happen? _____
   _____

5. Now use the facts you listed above to write the first paragraph of a news article about the event. Write complete sentences to give the reader all the details. Include a headline and draw a "photograph" in the box provided.

Writing an Explanatory Paragraph

An **explanatory paragraph** describes how something is done or how something works. Explanatory paragraphs often contain transitional words and expressions that help the reader follow the process being described. These include *next, now, then, however, likewise, similarly, again, first, last, finally, here, therefore, for example, in conclusion*, etc.

Think of something you are good at (e.g., shooting a layup in basketball, shopping for the perfect gift, writing a great letter) or a process you are familiar with (e.g., bathing an infant, cooking a certain dish). On the lines below, list the steps in the process.

_____

_____

_____

_____

_____

_____

Now write an explanatory paragraph about the topic you selected, using transitional words and expressions wherever necessary to help the reader understand the paragraph. Include a topic sentence and at least three supporting sentences.

_____

_____

_____

_____

_____

_____

_____

_____

_____

_____

_____

_____

Writing an Explanatory Paragraph (cont.)

Some explanatory paragraphs give very specific information about how to accomplish something. Explanatory paragraphs must be accurate, organized, and clear. The steps should be presented in the order in which they should be completed.

The recipe card below lists the ingredients for Pizza Surprise. On the lines provided, write a clear explanatory paragraph so that a reader could follow the recipe for this unusual dish. Don't worry—you won't have to eat the final product!

PIZZA SURPRISE

1 pre-made pizza crust
1 jar super spicy pizza sauce
2 cups shredded cheese
1 teaspoon salt
2 dashes garlic powder
1 dash oregano
1 teaspoon lime juice

1 handful of each of the following:
  pepperoni
  leftover meat loaf
  gummy worms
  pineapple
  mushrooms
  onions

_____
_____
_____
_____
_____
_____
_____
_____
_____
_____
_____
_____
_____
_____

Writing a Narrative Paragraph

A **narrative paragraph** tells a story. A good narrative paragraph contains plenty of interesting details.

Not Enough Detail: The stars were bright.
Interesting Details: The night sky looked as if a thousand fairies had just emptied jars of twinkle dust.

One strategy for writing exceptional narrative paragraphs is to *show*, not *tell*.

Tell: Marie was nervous.
Show: Marie couldn't hear anything the teacher was saying. Her legs felt like lead as she walked to the front of the classroom.

On the lines below, list the events that took place on either the best or the worst day of your life.

_____

_____

_____

_____

Now write a narrative paragraph about the day, and include as many interesting details as possible. Be sure to "show" rather than "tell" how you felt that day.

_____

_____

_____

_____

_____

_____

_____

_____

_____

_____

_____

Name _____

Writing a Persuasive Paragraph

A **persuasive paragraph** attempts to convince someone to do something or to believe something. In this type of paragraph, the topic sentence states an opinion and the supporting sentences provide reasons for accepting this view.

It is important to consider your audience when selecting reasons to include in a persuasive paragraph. Different reasons will be more persuasive for different audiences. For example, telling your parents you want your own car so you can go out with your friends more often would probably not persuade them to get you a car. A more persuasive reason might be to tell them that if you had a car you could drive your younger sisters to their after-school activities.

A good persuasive paragraph anticipates the main objection(s) to the opinion(s) presented, and provides information to eliminate that objection.

Example: You may be worried that I will not be able to pay for the car insurance, but I have already spoken to Mrs. Johnson about baby-sitting Joey every Sunday for extra money.

Imagine you have failed a very important algebra test. You have several good reasons for doing poorly on the test and you are going to write the math teacher, Mr. Hall, a letter requesting the opportunity to take the test again. Complete the following activities, and then begin your persuasive paragraph on the lines at the bottom of the page. (Continue your paragraph on the back of this paper.)

1. On the lines below, list five reasons that you failed the algebra test. Then number the reasons in order of importance.

   ____ _____
   ____ _____
   ____ _____
   ____ _____
   ____ _____

2. Write what you think Mr. Hall's main objection would be to allowing you to take the test again. _____
   _____

3. Write a good response to Mr. Hall's main objection.
   _____

Dear Mr. Hall,

_____
_____
_____

Evaluating a Paragraph

Read the following paragraph, and then complete the activities below.

"War" is a card game that involves several steps. First, a standard deck of cards is divided in half. Each of two players is given 26 cards. Next, each player places a card face up on the table. The player with the higher card wins both cards. This continues until the turned up cards are a pair. Then there is a "war." Three cards are added facedown by each player. Then a fourth card is turned over. Whoever turns over the higher card wins all the cards from that round. If the two new cards are a pair too, each player adds another card facedown and turns up a card. The game continues until one player wins all 52 cards. It can take a while.

1. What type of paragraph is this? _____

2. What is the topic sentence? _____

   _____

3. What type of sentence is the topic sentence (declarative, exclamatory, interrogative, or imperative)? _____

4. Underline a sentence that is in the passive voice.

5. Rewrite this sentence so that it is in the active voice. _____

   _____

6. Circle a pair of sentences that you think should be combined into one longer sentence.

7. Combine these sentences to make one sentence. _____

   _____

8. Rewrite the concluding sentence so that it clearly sums up the paragraph.

   _____

   _____

Name _____

Review

Place the letter of the correct definition on the line before each of the terms in the left column.

_____ 1. supporting detail

_____ 2. fragment

_____ 3. cause and effect paragraph

_____ 4. active voice

_____ 5. informative paragraph

_____ 6. compound sentence

_____ 7. narrative paragraph

_____ 8. interrogative sentence

_____ 9. descriptive paragraph

_____ 10. paragraph

_____ 11. persuasive paragraph

_____ 12. complete predicate

_____ 13. topic sentence

_____ 14. sentence

a. a sentence that asks a question

b. all of the words that tell what the subject is or does

c. a paragraph that presents the reasons for certain results or consequences

d. a group of words that expresses one complete thought and contains a subject and a predicate

e. a paragraph that tells a story

f. a sentence that states the main idea of a paragraph

g. a paragraph whose main purpose is to relate facts

h. a fact, example, statistic, or explanation that backs up the main idea of a paragraph

i. when the subject of the sentence performs the action

j. a sentence that is made up of two simple sentences joined by a comma and a connecting word

k. a paragraph that attempts to convince the reader to do something or to believe something

l. a paragraph that helps the reader clearly imagine what is being described

m. a sentence that is missing a subject, a predicate, or both

n. a group of sentences that develops one main idea